GRIEF ENTANGLEMENTS

Understanding Unresolved Grief and
What You Can Do About It

SHARON M. GREENLEE MS, RPC

CONTENTS

About the Author..v

Introduction vii

Short Personal Story ix

The Importance of Grief and the
Six Entanglements... I

What is *Healthy* Grief?... 5

The Entanglements... 9

Entanglement ONE: *Circumstances of the Death*...........................II

Reframing: A Useful Strategy to Use with
Entanglement ONE: Circumstances of the Death.........I3

The Writing Process or Journaling As a
Tool for Healing I7

Writing Strategy for Untangling from Entanglement ONE:
Circumstances of the Death..21

Entanglement TWO: *The Quality of the Relationship*...................27

Children Also Have Grief Entanglements:
JOEL'S story..33

ANNA'S Story:...37

Untangling from Entanglement TWO: The Quality of
the Relationship 43

Entanglement THREE: Unmet Needs of the Bereaved 49

Untangling from (or preventing) Entanglement THREE:
   Unmet Needs..55

Entanglement FOUR: Personal Sense of Identity
   Before and After the Loss of the Loved One 59

Untangling from Entanglement FOUR:
   Personal Sense of Identity 63

Entanglement FIVE: The Bereaved Person's
   Previous Reaction Pattern to Disappointment,
   Loss or Major Change 67

Untangling from Entanglement FIVE:
   The Bereaved Person's Previous Reaction
   Pattern to Disappointment, Loss, or
   Major Life Change. 73

Entanglement SIX: The Conscious or Unconscious
   Personal Need of the Bereaved to Prolong the
   Grief Process 79

Untangling from Entanglement SIX: The Conscious or
   Unconscious Personal Need of the Bereaved to
   Prolong the Grief Process...83

Ways to Avoid Grief Entanglements in the Future 85

AFTER CARE: Personal Thoughts From the Author........95

Acknowledgements 103

ABOUT THE AUTHOR

Sharon Greenlee is a registered professional counselor. She is also the mother of a son and stepson who were killed in separate automobile accidents on the same day. This tragedy, the loss of two grandchildren, and the unresolved childhood grief she carried from the loss of her mother became the beginning of a deep and dark grief journey.

Sharon's story is touching and optimistic. From her willingness to meet despair rather than be taken in by it, she has been able to find peace and resolve from her losses and to move forward professionally to help others recognize situations that can cause *them* to become *stuck* in their grief. She refers to these situations or issues as *the six entanglements*. This book is for anyone who has suffered the loss of a loved one or wishes to have a better understanding of grief and recovery.

INTRODUCTION

*As a grief therapist and one who has experienced deep
personal loss, I dedicate this work to you, the reader.*

People pick up a book like this for different reasons. Maybe
you have recently lost a loved one. If so, I am truly sorry for
your loss. I am sure that the very fabric of your existence feels
altered and worn right now … especially if the person who
died was one of the main threads of your life.

If you were drawn to open this book because you have a friend or
a loved one who recently lost someone of significance, I know how
heavy the burden can feel as you try to help hold the sadness and
sorrow of someone close to you. We often feel helpless in knowing
what to say or what to do to help a grieving friend or loved one.

Whatever your situation, it is my genuine wish that this book
may be helpful to you at this time. I believe it is no coinci-
dence that we are meeting today!

You may wish to read all of the text before attempting any of the self-help suggestions that follow each of the six grief entanglements. On the other hand you may encounter a section that applies to your immediate situation and you may prefer to settle your thinking right there for a bit. In this case you would probably benefit from doing the follow-up exercise(s) for that specific grief entanglement right away.

I can almost assure you that if you are presently living with unsettled and/or unresolved grief and it has been over a year or eighteen months since the loss of your loved one, you will find some answers and some hope in the pages ahead.

SHORT PERSONAL STORY

When I was eleven years old my mother died suddenly. I learned quickly the sharp and painful feelings of loss and sorrow. With no father for support and two grandparents grieving for their only child, I wandered my thoughts aimlessly and alone, much the same as one might wander alone through a strange, dark and narrow alley. I couldn't find my way through, or out of the darkness and I didn't know who to ask for directions.

In naïve attempts to restore life and joy for my grandmother, who was the only remaining face of security and stability left in my life, I buried sorrow and sadness and covered grief with a thin, invisible veil that seemed at the time to fool everyone … including me!

It would be many years later when my husband Richard and I would lose both of our oldest sons, in separate accidents on the same day that I would learn that there would be no more veiling grief, no more denying, no more running away.

The long and tumultuous inner grief journey as well as numerous and unusual events that followed the death of our sons would carry me into and through a very painful, though ultimately peaceful resolve. And, though highly unexpected, I would eventually be led to help others in *their* deepest moments of sorrow. From this would come a clear and pristine life-lesson: *Each time we extend our hands and our heart to someone who is suffering, another layer of our own sorrow washes away!*

THE IMPORTANCE
OF GRIEF

During the long process of doing my own grief work, as well as spending time with others in the clinical setting, I am reminded over and again that there is not one single or correct way to grieve. Whereas, there may be similarities in how we think about and process our individual losses, it is clear that each loss carries its own grief story. How one interprets the details of the story will be the greatest variable regarding how each individual resolves or does not resolve the loss.

The *details* of the grief stories have become the focus of my work. In listening to hundreds of stories, six sets of story patterns emerge repeatedly. These patterns involve circumstances or issues that may cause the grieving person to have difficulty resuming a fully healthy or contented lifestyle after the loss of a loved one. I refer to each story pattern as an *entanglement* because of the capacity of each situation or issue to cloud the grief healing process. One or more of the *six entanglements* may be responsible for, and are capable of, propelling a person into a lingering and unresolved grief, referred to by some as being *stuck* in the grief.

Grief, at its best (if there can be such a thing) can be so bitterly painful and seemingly endless that one does not need to endure the added torment that usually accompanies *entangled* grief. The six entanglements are:

1. The Circumstances of the Death;
2. The Quality of the Relationship(s);
3. The Unmet Needs of the Bereaved;
4. The Sense of Identity of the Bereaved Before and After the Loss;
5. The Bereaved Person's Personal Reaction Pattern to Loss or Major Life Change;
6. The Conscious or Unconscious Personal Need of the Bereaved to Prolong the Grief Process.

After reading about each entanglement, you will readily recognize if one or more apply to your grief situation. It is important to keep in mind that many people are able to experience the deep sadness and sorrow connected with the loss of a loved one without having a grief entanglement involved.

On the other hand, some people experience one or more of the six situations after the loss of a loved one and are able to work through the related problems without having things progress to entanglement proportion. Other bereaved individuals may have one or more, or possibly all six situations and realize that they are in the midst of an entangled, prolonged and agonizing grief experience. Before I explain the six entanglements, let's define *healthy* grief.

WHAT IS *HEALTHY* GRIEF?

When I speak of *healthy* grief, I am referring to the grieving individual who has lost a loved one and may be going through one of the worst experiences of his or her life, yet this person will do so in a way that will ultimately lead to a sense of peace and resolve. In most every case of *healthy* grief, the grieving person will ultimately integrate the loss of the loved one into his or her everyday life. It does not mean that the bereaved ceases to miss or stop thinking of the loved one. On the contrary, *healthy* grief can carry with it months or possibly years of experiencing the return of tears when a certain song plays or when a loving experience with the missed one is recalled. All of this thinking goes with what I call the *earthly miss* and it is very normal.

Healthy grief includes the ability to:
- mourn the loss of the loved one;
- forgive and give up old resentments that might have been present in the relationship between the bereaved and the one who died;

- recall and preserve the happy times;
- find comfort and respite in the love and fellowship of relatives and friends at least part of the time;
- be willing to take time to be alone with one's thoughts, as this can definitely be a *sorting out* time;
- after a length of time, return to a basically happy and productive life, feeling reasonably assured that parts of life can be okay again, while acknowledging that things will never be exactly as they were before.
- finally find comfort and peace in the loving memories of the one who died.

Healthy grief does mean that you are taking the time to go to the bottom of your sorrow and sadness and to listen to all that resonates there. *Healthy grief* also means that you allow yourself to discover if one or more of the entanglements are involved in your particular situation and that you are willing to take the time to resolve and *untangle* thoughts and issues that may otherwise keep you stuck in your grief.

Finally, *healthy grief* carries with it a knowing that the love sustained from this person when you were together will continue to sustain you, in a different way, even though you are now apart.

One would not be experiencing *healthy* grief if the bereaved:

- is depressed and/or overly saddened, absorbed and distraught with the loss over a long and extended period of time (eighteen months or longer) and to the extent that it continues to interfere with normal life functioning;
- feels inadequate in being able to change interfering feelings and perceptions.

If either of these characteristics *speak* to your grief experience or that of a bereaved loved one, it would be advisable to seek assistance in working through any unresolved issues.

THE
ENTANGLEMENTS

ENTANGLEMENT ONE: CIRCUMSTANCES OF THE DEATH

How the death occurs has a great impact on grief and healing. Each death scenario carries its own dynamics. A few dramatic examples include the trauma of violent death, death by suicide, natural disasters that result in death, the loss of a newborn, or the death of a child in a home accident to name only a few.

Obviously, every death has a cause or circumstance. When the circumstances of the death carry with it a major and dramatic theme, there is the potential or even probability that the grief may become of entanglement proportion.

In almost every instance, dealing with the emotions that go with certain causes of death is a heroic action in itself. For example, try to fathom the emotional experiences of a mother who recently lost her third and last son in a gang shooting. Not only is the mother engulfed in sorrow, she is confronted with a myriad of feelings, among them possibly anger or even hatred towards the perpetrators of the crime.

And one can hardly imagine the emotions surrounding the rape and murder of a little girl or of a human being of any age for that matter. And how does one handle the emotions that must come with losing a loved one who has contracted AIDS from a trusted other? All of the feelings and emotions surrounding the death, regardless of cause, will have to be acknowledged and faced before such horrendous loss can even begin to find resolve.

In summary, this first entanglement is probable when sudden and unexpected death occurs, especially when it involves intrusive and dramatic or traumatic circumstances. In these cases, the bereaved is left to deal with much more than the heartbreaking loss of the loved one. Unresolved feelings and emotions may seem endless and knowing that each one must be confronted is its own courageous battle. This entanglement almost promises a more prolonged and anguish-filled grief period. The bereaved would be wise to seek the help of a qualified professional for at least a short period of time.

REFRAMING: A USEFUL STRATEGY TO USE WITH ENTANGLEMENT ONE: CIRCUMSTANCES OF THE DEATH

Use *Reframing* As a Means to Keep the Happy Memories and Dim the Negative Ones: A Technique for *Changing Images in the Mind*

Mayo Clinic uses the term, *complicated grief* to describe any unusual grief circumstances. How a loved one dies certainly can make the grief and recovery more complicated and can easily move to *entangled* proportions.

The goal of cognitive restructuring or *reframing* is to allow the bereaved person ways of changing and replacing negative and seemingly unforgettable images or pictures that collect in the mind. Having the ability to do this can be especially significant when dealing with the manner in which the loved one died.

Unusual and horrific death situations are capable of leaving lingering and harmful images in the minds of the bereaved. Events such as the 911 New York City terrorist attack and the Katrina tsunami are examples. Equally important and significant would be any loss of a loved one who may have suffered extreme and traumatic circumstances at the time of his or her death. Many wartime losses fit into this category.

It is not uncommon for dark images to play repeatedly in the mind of the bereaved and when this occurs, it can be difficult to find escape or peace of mind and it definitely is capable of causing entangled and lingering grief.

The following strategy was developed when working with a close friend whose son had been killed in a horrendous car accident. Her son's body had been injured beyond recognition. She was haunted by the thoughts of his injuries and what his final moments of life might have been like. Each time she thought of him, the horrible imaginative images surfaced all over again. By practicing the following strategy each time the negative images appeared, she was eventually able to change her thoughts and finally gain some sense of peace.

Activity for *Changing Pictures In the Mind:*

"Close your eyes and allow your mind to sort through numerous loving and happy times and events with your loved one. Allow yourself to feel whatever sadness, sorrow or smiles that might go with your thoughts but try to stay connected to collecting the good memories.

"Begin by choosing one specific fond memory and make a picture of your loved one in your mind as it relates to the memory. 'See' what the person might be wearing; visualize the facial expression of your loved one. See the picture as vividly as if your mind were a camera capturing this image for all time. (Example: My friend saw her son wearing his red plaid flannel shirt, coming through the door at home calling out, "Hey, where is everyone?" She keeps this as her number One picture.

You will be collecting five different positive images of your loved one. It's easiest to keep the images in the same order each time by associating each image with one of your four fingers and thumb. Mentally place (associate) the first image on your thumb.

"Collect your second image and fond memory of your loved one. This one might be associated with an entirely different time period. The important thing is that the visual be very clear in your mind. When you have your second image, make an association by placing this second picture on your first (pointy) finger.

"Continue this process as you collect five images. Each new image will go on a different finger. Remember to keep the same picture/finger association. For example, the image of her son coming through the door is always held on her thumb."

If and when a negative or hurtful image of your loved one appears in your mind, gently ask yourself to *"Stop the thought"* and immediately replace that image with the mental *roll of film* you have created. Always see the picture images in the same original order and always remember the association you have created on your fingers.

Slowly but surely the hurtful images will dim as you continue to replace negative, hurtful thoughts with the five picture memories that you have created as replacements. Trust, that over time you will be able to feel the presence of your loved one as you want to remember him or her. Eventually you may even feel the comfort that this little ritual can bring.

(Taken in part from an article by Sharon Greenlee, for a publication titled, *No One Should See What I Have Seen:* A book for those who have experienced terrifying and horrific tragedy. A Centering Corporation Resource, 2002).

THE WRITING PROCESS OR JOURNALING AS A TOOL FOR HEALING

In the many years I have been journaling and teaching this process to others, I continue to look for ways to help myself and others excavate the far corners of the mind when looking for one's deepest truths and answers. Knowing there is not a *one-size-fits-all* writing process, you may wish to give the technique I describe a try and later adjust it to whatever fits best for you. Many of us are not entirely comfortable writing our deeper and possibly less than desirable thoughts and ideas in a beautiful leather bound journal. That was certainly the case for me when I received my first journal gift many years ago and tried to pour all of my thoughts into that beautiful golden edged journal filled with Kahil Gibran quotes. It took a long time to gain courage to post my most hurtful thoughts onto those beautiful pages and after doing so, I ended up stapling pages together if the words seemed too bold or shameful. I could barely stand to reread the words myself, let alone wonder what someone else would think should they pick up my journal. During this period in my life, I was trying to gain better self-understanding as well as trying to grasp the meaning attached to the short relationship I had with my mother, who suddenly died when I was eleven. Excavating the childhood memories was unsettling to say the least and to place such thoughts onto the page of such a beautiful book was more than I could continue to do. Instead, I would write in a plain spiral notebook so that I could tear out the pages and throw them away. It would be some time before I would begin writing in a *real* journal again.

Today I suggest to my clients and workshop participants a technique I have used since my first journal experience. During the initial *excavation* of thoughts and feelings, use a yellow legal pad or a spiral notebook or something that you won't mind throwing away when you finish your initial *write*. Allow yourself to *dump* all of your thoughts onto the page quickly and without censorship. Read what you have written and destroy it. It is normal and human to feel many different and possibly uncomfortable feelings and emotions when thinking and writing about certain relationships or past experiences. Keep in mind that all of our thoughts deserve to be honored and understood. And, it is all the more reason for bringing these feelings to your awareness so that you can possibly do something productive with them. It is also a reason not to keep the pages! Some of what we think and write has the potential to be hurtful or harmful to someone else. That is not our intention. Keeping the pages only takes unnecessary energy from you, wondering where you put them, asking yourself if they are safe and on and on. Get rid of them!

This is where your *other* journal comes in handy. Choose for yourself an attractive spiral-bound journal to record the lessons you have learned from the *dump book* writing. This will allow you to recall thoughts that went into your dump book and yet encourage you to realize how far you have come in knowing and accepting more of your honest self. I refer to this journal as my *Beauty Book* because it contains the lessons and knowledge I've gained from using the *dump* process. I also call it that because I love to insert short poetry pieces that hold meaning for me, or bits of my own original verse. Sometimes I doodle and decorate the pages or add a colorful or decorative flower or design. My *beauty book* feels very personal and reminds me that I'm truly capable of not only owning some of my more challenging thoughts and situations, I am capable of finding answers and some peaceful resolve.

As final words of encouragement if you decide to pursue or extend the personal writing I describe, please remind yourself that life is simply too short to spend in endless inner turmoil and conflict. Writing can be a wonderful catharsis and processing your writing with a qualified and trusted other can be just as helpful. Be patient with yourself as you work through your feelings that are connected with the circumstances of the death of your loved one, or whatever you happen to be writing about. In this case, it's important to remember that you are dealing with two separate issues: the sorrow and sadness of losing your loved one as well as the means in which the loved one died.

WRITING STRATEGY FOR UNTANGLING FROM ENTANGLEMENT ONE: CIRCUMSTANCES OF THE DEATH

Writing is an excellent process for being in touch with the deepest self. The writing process allows for an extended, internal awareness of one's personal story or issue to begin to unfold. Answers to issues, previously less understood, will become more apparent and greater self-understanding will take place. Questions that still need answers will be like doors waiting to be opened in order to move forward and out of the untangled grief. Even though this writing suggestion is directed to Entanglement One, consider writing as a means of bringing forth knowledge, feelings and emotions regardless of the entanglement involved in your grief.

Some may not find writing to be a useful tool, though many people use that excuse when in fact, it is the discomfort and emotional pain that often, or usually, accompanies the task. This too is normal! To work through this process might mean gaining courage to claim your strongest self and give it more than a single try.

Writing activity:

I. Make a list of everything that comes to your mind as it relates to your story, for example:
- The shock of the sudden diagnosis;
- The surgery was so invasive;
- Watching her suffer in spite of the attempted pain management;
- The trauma of cleaning her surgical wounds (unsightly, painful);
- The news that hospice was the only alternative;
- Watching her die and feeling so helpless and sad

2. Write all of your deepest thoughts regarding *The Circumstances of the Death* of the loved one. Include the time building up to the time of the death as well as any circumstances right after the death that may have been unusually troublesome. In other words, retell your story on paper.

3. As you write, many and varied emotions will begin to emerge. You may feel anger, guilt, blame, fear, resentment,

or any other multitude of emotions that go with your story. Avoid resisting or judging as it could be one or more of these feelings that have been standing in the way of you moving forward. Continue using this simple writing technique as it will allow you to look further into your interior.

I. Draw a small circle and divide it into four quadrants.

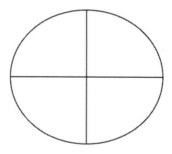

2. In each quarter of the circle write a single word that describes the strongest feelings or emotions attached to *the circumstances of the death* of the loved one.

Example:

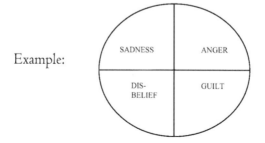

3. Choose the word that *speaks* to you and begin writing as quickly as you can, beginning with the phrase: *"I feel*_____ or, *"I felt*_____when _____. Write for as long as you need to in order to *empty* your thoughts and feelings in regard to this emotion. If your thoughts *change gears* as you write, allow it to happen and if tears need to spill forth, allow that to happen as well. Trust the process, trust yourself and keep writing!

When finished, read what you have written and be aware of new thoughts or feelings that may have surfaced during or after the writing. It may feel comfortable processing any new thoughts or emotions on your own. On the other hand, you may find more comfort and assurance by discussing your thoughts with a grief counselor or a trusted friend or family member. Because this writing exercise has the potential of arousing emotions, you may wish to wait until another time before addressing the other words in your circle. Or, you may have enough answers for right now and you will wait for another day and repeat the exercise using the feelings and emotions that surface on that particular day.

To further illustrate what one can discover through such writing, let's use *Mary's* situation as the circle of words above belong to her. She circled and wrote about *guilt.* After her friend *Jan's* serious cancer surgery, Mary's responsibility, as a close friend and caregiver, was to cleanse and dress Jan's surgical wounds three times a day. The cleansing procedure was invasive and painful for Jan and yet she was encouraging and grateful to Mary for helping her. Mary's sadness and distress at simply having to witness the condition of Jan's wounds, let alone cleanse them was almost more than she could endure. At the same time she felt guilt and shame for not wanting to do it and for not being stronger in the situation. Though she knew she would never turn away from her friend, she continued to dread the three-times-a-day procedure. In spite of all of the hopes and dreams, Jan never recovered and the grief of losing her was shocking and raw for all who loved her. Each time Mary thought about Jan, the visual of her beloved friend and her horrible wounds came back into Mary's mind, followed by the guilt.

In an attempt to calm and clarify her feelings, Mary used writing to gain a deeper understanding of the situation. She was able to see that caring for Jan would have been difficult for any non-medical person. She also realized that she had felt total love and compassion for Jan and would need to find some of the same feeling for herself.

With the help of a grief counselor, Mary learned how to reframe thoughts and pictures in her mind so as to replace the gruesome experience of Jan's last days with some of the more beautiful times they had shared together. Over time, Mary was able to separate her grief feelings from the tangled emotions of guilt and inadequacy that she felt in the role of caregiver. This story is a reminder that once things are *untangled,* there will still be grief and sadness, though *time* will offer respite and reprieve.

ENTANGLEMENT TWO:
THE QUALITY OF THE RELATIONSHIP

When ill-feelings between the bereaved and his or her loved one have been resolved, and when the final parting has been congenial and loving, in spite of the sadness, a sense of peace and comfort can eventually claim a resting spot in the mind and heart of the one who grieves.

When unresolved anger, guilt, disappointment, conflict or other negative feelings and emotions have existed between the bereaved and the deceased, or between the bereaved and another person in close relationship with the one who died (doctor, friend, relative, etc.), the grief process can become more complicated, frustrated and prolonged. And the results can be an entangled grief that can cause one to become emotionally *stuck*. *Joe* and *Maggie's* open and loving relationship is a perfect example of why entanglement two will never be an issue for Joe.

In spite of Joe's sorrow over the loss of his beloved Maggie, he finds a sense of peace and comfort. *"Sometimes I think I can't go on without her"*, he shares during his first support group meeting. In later sessions as he listens to others and joins in discussion he looks even closer at his relationship with Maggie. Tears form as he reminisces about their special love and communication. *"We were honest with one another and we always took care of each other's feelings. Oh, we had our little spats like everyone but we were never really ugly to each other."* His eyes reflect the loving memories as he finishes. *"We always made up before the ten o'clock news was over."* Recalling their special bond, Joe's focus moves from what he no longer has with Maggie to the treasured memories he will hold forever. He has no regrets for things he did or did not say to her. Though he will continue to miss Maggie and grieve her absence, their relationship was complete and healthy. Joe will not be tormented with things he wishes he had or had not done or said. The second entanglement will not be mixed into his grief.

On the other hand, Dee's story helps us understand how a less than ideal relationship with oneself and the one who died can cause extra and prolonged anguish:

Though Dee's mother was killed suddenly in an automobile collision over five years prior to our first session, Dee was obviously still devastated over the loss. She sobbed as she recounted the tragic day. *"It's as if it were yesterday,"* she said. She explained that she had never been able to tell her mother goodbye and wondered if that accounted for the on-going grief that continually lived in the back of her mind. Dee continued by explaining that due to the extent of her mother's injuries from the accident, the casket remained closed before and during the funeral service. Dee had heard that being unable to view the body could also cause a lack of grief closure. *"Do you think this is why I can't get over this?"* she asked.

As she related simple facts about her mother, she recalled, *"My mother was strong and determined. She liked her way and was a bit of a perfectionist. She did everything well and taught me many of the things she knew. I caught on quickly and I always felt like her favorite when I was little."*

During our second session Dee seemed ready to go deeper regarding the relationship she had established with her mother as an adult. *"She was so angry when I married Ted. She thought he wasn't good enough. Of course, she never liked anyone I brought home. I don't think she wanted me to marry anyone! She didn't even come to our wedding and I cried secretly for days. As I think about it, when I married Ted, the relationship with my mom died. I kept trying to make things right. She would never forgive or accept me in the same way after that. Before I got the courage to go see her and try to work it out, she had the accident and died."*

Through words and tears Dee discovered important information that formed links between the unresolved relationship with her mother and the entanglement that kept her stuck in her grief.

Over the next two sessions Dee was able to openly acknowledge, understand and accept that it was normal for her to long for her mother's approval and at the same time feel resentful and angry for her passive aggressive, controlling actions. Dee spoke of beginning to feel *"free."*

"I think I felt as bad about never getting to tell Mom how I felt about how she treated me and Ted as I did about her dying. When she died it was like she still had the last word and won! Now I know she didn't need to win and I don't need to either. To know that is really freeing!"

Dee had spent most of her life trying to live up to her mother's expectations. She was successful in that venture until she married Ted. Because her mother continued to try to control Dee by rejecting Ted and the marriage, Dee felt helpless as well as resentful. She admitted always trying to gain outside approval from others and always wishing she had it from her mother. The final and most seething rejection came when Dee's mother died quickly and unexpectedly. There was still too much *unfinished business* left between Dee and her mother. Her tangled feelings of love, anger, hurt and rejection stood in the way of Dee being able to express clear and sincere feelings of loss. Once she was able to openly express her anger and resentment without guilt, she was better able to forgive her mother's misguided behaviors.

In her final session, Dee wrote a letter to her mother expressing all of the things she had wanted to say when her mother was alive. It didn't really matter that her mother couldn't read the letter. It was enough for Dee to simply express herself openly and with honesty. Her final goal was to forgive her mother and to accept what she could not forgive. Although not a storybook ending, this adult daughter was able to separate from the control of her mother and let go of anger and resentment and finally find a more peaceful ending to her grief story.

CHILDREN ALSO HAVE GRIEF ENTANGLEMENTS
MORE ABOUT ENTANGLEMENT TWO: THE QUALITY OF THE RELATIONSHIP

Joel's Story:

Joel was nine when his mother brought him to see me. His experience shows how feelings of guilt can stand in the way of resolving childhood grief. *"Joel seems more and more depressed as time passes since his grandpa's death,"* his mother shared. She described Joel and Grandpa as, *"buddies who spent a great deal of time together."*

During our first session, Joel's tone was sad, though he seemed to want to talk about his Grandpa. *"He was funny and always took me places. We did lots of things together. Everybody liked him."*

Later in the same session, Joel spoke of his grandpa's alcoholism and told me in a soft voice, *"Grandpa died of liver disease."* I showed Joel a chart with six different feelings written on it. I asked him to choose one word that might best express how someone might feel after someone dies. Joel pointed to the word *guilt*. Eyes brimming with tears, he said that he thought it was a lot his fault that his grandpa died.

"Whenever I went to Grandpa's house, I ALWAYS asked for soda," Joel related in a tone of self-disgust. Grandpa always said, *'Sure!'* We'd go to the *frig* and Grandpa would act like he was getting two sodas, but he'd always put one back and say, *'I guess I'll have me a nip of my good stuff instead.'"*

"And then he'd reach for his Jimmy Beam," Joel explained tearfully.

"If I hadn't been such a selfish boy and always asked for soda, maybe Grandpa wouldn't have died."

Joel sobbed uncontrollably. My response was simply to touch his arm gently. On this day I was working with Joel in my home office. I asked him to do a role-play with me, in hopes that he might see the conversation between him and his grandfather more clearly and from another perspective. He was willing to try. I assumed the role of Joel and he played the part of his grandpa.

I asked for soda and assuming Grandpa's role, Joel said, *"Sure, let's go get it."* We even walked to the refrigerator in the kitchen. When we got to the part where Grandpa reaches for two sodas and puts one back, Joel hesitated. And when Joel reached for

the imaginary bourbon bottle, he said, *"I guess I'll have a nip . . ."*
He stopped, with what seemed to be a sudden realization, and
broke into tears. *"I didn't do it to him. He did it to himself! He didn't
have to put the soda back. He didn't have to take the Jimmy Beam. HE did
it to himself!"* This time, Joel's sobs were therapeutic and healing.

It was simply good fortune that the role-play was so successful
and happened during his first session. The experience allowed
Joel to have a more accurate perception of the situation. It
will be normal for Joel to continue missing his grandfather.
He will naturally feel sadness and probably still experience
tears knowing that the two of them can no longer do the
things they used to do together. The difference is that these
are expressions of *healthy grief*, and a normal part of the grief
process.

We talked of the many good memories the two of them had
together and he captured some of them in drawings. Joel will
now be able to keep those memories, as well as recall the lessons regarding *choices* that Grandpa ultimately taught him.

ANNA'S STORY

Note: Anna's story is less about Entanglement Two specifically, yet it illustrates how the pre-school age child might be helped through a traumatic grief situation.

Young children have varying concepts and understanding of grief based upon their age and emotional development. Anna's story helps illustrate how grief, though not completely understood by the very young child, can nonetheless, be filled with pain and sadness.

This is actually two stories…Anna's and mine… and the story begins in my eleventh year when my mother died. Being witness to my grandmother's grief from the loss of her only child emotionally overwhelmed me! To see and hear her wailing was a heartbreaking and frightening experience. Her sadness, and my inability to do anything about it grieved me, possibly as much as the grief I felt for the loss of my mother.

My grandmother had been my emotional haven. I felt totally alone and helpless!

The words that my uncle spoke to me on the night my mother died: *"be strong for your grandmother because now you are all she has"* rested in the center of my heart and I dearly believed that what he said was true. I promised myself that I would not only be strong for her, I would be good and do all I could to cheer her. My second promise to myself was not to cry or be sad in front of her. A good counselor could have shown me how inappropriate it was to make such a promise to anyone, let alone to myself.

Searching for any kind of escape, I would crawl into the closet and bury myself deep among my mother's clothes. In this quiet, dark sanctuary I could be with her, smell her, remember her and even feel a bit of comfort. This was the only place I knew where I could allow the quiet sobs to release… sobs that I could no longer control.

With this being the fabric of my strongest childhood grief memory, how might I ever have predicted or prepared myself for what would happen when I became a mother? When the phone call came that November night, telling me of my son's automobile accident and instant death, my heart was pierced with an overwhelming pain of familiar intensity. Hearing the news that Dave had been killed overwhelmed even the childhood message of my mother's death.

Flying from Wyoming back to Iowa, my mind was filled with scenes and scenarios of Dave: the sweet-smelling, toe-headed baby that I so loved to hold and cuddle in a towel right after his bath. The fun-loving, curious toddler, ...the smile on his face and the shirt he wore to his first seventh grade dance. Images of him filled my mind, knowing at the same time I would never see him again. My next thoughts were of Dave's two small children. Anna was three and Andy was twenty-two months. Was there any possible way to help them in ways no one had known to help me?

Upon landing in Des Moines, I went immediately to the children and their mother. Anna was quiet, no usual smiles and she only spoke in a soft voice to tell me that her tummy wouldn't stop hurting. Andy kept saying, *"Daddy's at work! Daddy's at work!"* Anna turned to him and in a loud voice cried out, *"NO, Andy! Daddy's not at work. Daddy died just like Shuka died!"* (their dog had been hit by a car the week before).

Thoughts of my childhood loss came flooding back and I prayed to know of something to do or say to help these precious children who were grieving, each in their own way.

A sudden thought came into my mind. Writing had been my salvation as I was growing up. I kept a diary or journal much of my life and as a first grade teacher I had integrated each child's personal stories into the reading process. A child would sit with me and tell any story he or she wished to share. I would write the story, and in the process, the child would see that *reading* was simply *talking* on paper. I called these *"Talk-a-Stories"* and the children loved them. I would try such a story with Anna. She was highly verbal for her age.

We sat together at the big kitchen table. I told her we were going to make a story about Daddy and when we finished, her tummy might feel better. (Please know those words were based only on a prayerful hunch). She seemed excited to do this, and I began: *"Tell me everything you remember about Daddy!"*

Her eyes responded first and she immediately became more animated as she started telling one thing and then another about her daddy. I wrote as fast as I could and suddenly she stopped, saying, *"That's all!"* After exchanging a few words and a hug, she ran outside to her swing set. Within two minutes she was back and saying, *"There's More!"* She remembered one thing and then another. I wrote every word just as she said it. When she finished, the only editing I did was to put sentences that talked about the same subject (example: her reference to daddy and cooking) together. Otherwise, the story is just as she told it. This is Anna's story:

Anna's Talk-a-Story, at the age of three years and three months, as told to her Grammie Sharon:

"I remember Daddy. He always called me Sugarfoot! I remember the fun things I liked to do with him. I liked to go to Edmunson Park with Daddy.

We played on the swings and went on the merry-go-round. When it stopped we went to the horsies or the slide. Dad would watch us, and he laughed. One time he took Andy and me down the BIG, BIG (words exaggerated) slide. When we went down, down, Daddy said, 'WHEE-EE-EE."

"*At home, me and Daddy and Andy sat and read books. Daddy read books and then we ate supper. Daddy cooked me good things to eat. He cooked vegetable soup and meat loaf too. At Christmas time, when I was two, Daddy and me dipped pretzels. Daddy took me swimming at the Y and at the motel. We had lots of fun. When we were at the motel, I almost missed the step and fell in the water. It was fun.*"

(Anna is pensive and quiet...deep in thought and then she continues) "*I remember about Daddy. Andy used to put his toys on the heater and Daddy would say, 'No, No!'*" (Anna quotes Daddy's 'no-no' imitating Dave's soft, gentle tone.)

"*When we would come home, Daddy would always call, 'IS ANYBODY HOME?'*" (She uses a lyrical voice, imitating Dave's tone).

"*Andy asks, 'When's Daddy coming back?' I tell him, "Daddy got killed. Daddy died just like Shuka died. They both got killed." Andy says, 'No sir. Daddy's at work.'* She looks over at Andy and says, "*Andy, I wish he would come home, too. I would like to do the fun things I used to do with Daddy.*"

As I stood at the door, ready to go back to town that evening, I realized that my own familiar, childhood ache that I felt inside...the ache that Anna was trying to describe, had started to subside. Anna wasn't talking about a tummy ache either. And the next thing that happened was enough to make the angels smile.

Beautiful little Anna pulled a chair up to the kitchen table across from where Andy was sitting. She had a pencil and paper in front of her as she said, *"Okay, Andy, tell me EVERYTHING you remember about Daddy."*

Author's Note: This personal work with Anna and Andy was the beginning of a long journey of helping children in grief. As a mental health professional I have been invited into many schools and classrooms after the death of a student or staff member and worked with children individually as well as in the classroom setting. In this process I have listened to hundreds of children's grief stories and each time my own healing becomes a bit more complete.

The three real-life scenarios regarding Dee and her mother, Joel and his grandpa, and Anna's story about her daddy, illustrate how a grief therapist might be helpful after the loss of a loved one.

UNTANGLING FROM ENTANGLEMENT TWO: THE QUALITY OF THE RELATIONSHIP

One of the best ways to help yourself is to be willing to be in touch with ALL of your feelings as they relate to ALL of the people connected to your grief story. Ask yourself, *"Regarding my grief story, who are the people with whom I feel 'out of sorts' right now?"*

1.Create a list, *web* or *mind-map*. *Webbing* or *mind-mapping* is a quick and easy, abbreviated technique that offers a way to see words or thoughts in a quick, clear and random manner rather than in a long, thought out, sequenced form. Name each of the people involved in your story on separate strands of the web. (Figure I).

Here is an example:

Figure 1. (Example)

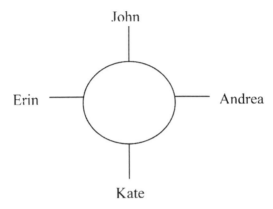

2. Create new strands out from each name that tell how you feel in relationship to this person at the present time. You will have best results if you do not withhold thoughts and feelings and simply let your thoughts flow honestly and uncensored.

Figure 2. (Example)

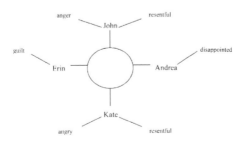

3. As a final step, write a few paragraphs regarding each person you have named on your web and explain to yourself why you have these feelings toward the person. Explore how having these feelings has effected you. Are you satisfied to keep feeling the way you do right now? Who or what might help you deal with these feelings? What needs to change? What do you have control over in making things different?

We can see from this example that by not censoring our thoughts we are able to gain a more clear understanding of our true perceptions of the other person as well as how we are personally reacting to the perceptions. In this illustration, as well as in real-life scenarios, the bereaved and entangled person will usually uncover true feelings that might otherwise be masked or unclear. For example, feelings of anger often mask other deeper feelings of hurt and/or fear. This short writing technique usually results in greater insight and self-understanding.

You may be asking, *"So, what do I do with all of this information now that I seem to have a bit more insight into my feelings?"*

1) This may be the time you wish to share your thinking with a reputable, grief therapist who should be able to listen with empathy and hopefully offer further insight, support, and direction.

2) Write a letter to the person or people involved. Know ahead of time that you will **NOT** send the letter! This is an opportunity to say what you want

to say without the worry or concern of escalat-
ing, or taking the situation in a direction that may
be unhealthy for all concerned. Think of it as a
harmless, yet healthy *emptying* technique. Read your
letter out loud and then destroy it.

Finally, take a few deep breaths. As you breathe in, imagine
you are taking in peaceful and loving energy from the universe.
As you *exhale*, visualize yourself letting go of each thought or
idea that has been causing you extra grief and unhappiness.
Listen to each breath. Be aware of the tension and heaviness
that is leaving your body as you *let go* of this burden of strong
emotions. Repeat this well-known and excellent emotional
cleansing technique at least twice a day. If you have trouble
doing this alone, by all means work with a professional as he
or she will understand the depth of your problem and should
do everything possible to help you find resolve. If lack of for-
giveness is a key issue, keep in mind that it actually takes more
energy to hold on to old grudges than to forgive and move on.
A sweet emotional freedom takes place when one chooses to
forgive even if it takes giving up the hurt or resentment again
and again. Develop a personal mantra to say everyday. It may
go something like mine:

"Love, Forgive,
Trust, Let Go!"

These words are powerful and when repeated over time, will help change the direction of your life! Though it sounds so simple, it is SO true!

ENTANGLEMENT THREE: *UNMET NEEDS OF THE BEREAVED AS A RESULT OF THE DEATH OF THE LOVED ONE*

Unmet Needs is possibly the most common of the entangle-ments. Examples of real-life stories involving *unmet needs* of bereaved individuals will best illustrate this entanglement.

At the age of thirty-eight *Tim* thought his life with *Molly* and their three children was as good as it could get. One can only imagine his shock, disbelief and grief when she died suddenly one summer morning of a heart attack while working out with a friend.

Tim came to counseling seven months after his wife died, sharing that he was sinking deeper in despair as the weeks went by. Even with the help of his mother and mother-in-law,

Tim was exhausted at the end of the day and found himself being comforted more and more by the bourbon bottle. He missed Molly's smile, her hugs and physical comfort and he missed having a mother for his children and a wife for himself.

"She did so many things for us," he began. *"She loved to cook and bake and the kitchen always smelled good. I don't know… she just kept things nice around here. My mom bakes for us and I have a cleaning lady so I don't have to do that! It still isn't anywhere near the same."* His eyes reflected the meaning of his words.

"I miss our walks in the evening. I've been trying to do that with the kids, but it's just not the same without her, though it does give me a chance to be with the girls. I can't imagine what this is like for my girls and I know I'm not there for them like I should be."

As Tim spoke, it was clear that he was trying to make sense out of all that had happened and even possibly trying to encourage himself with the assurance that he was working hard to try to make things as normal as possible.

As the conversation unfolded, in spite of hearing all of the things he was trying to do to *mend the cracks and fill in the blanks* regarding the many things that Molly did for the family, it seemed that there was something else that Tim had not yet uncovered for himself. His grief story appeared to hold more than the normal *earthly miss* and there definitely seemed to be an even more serious *unmet need* that was causing an entanglement.

When asked if he could pinpoint the time or times when he experienced his deepest grief, he was thoughtful for a time and looked up, shaking his head slightly as if in disbelief.

"This feels absurd", he said. "Yes! At night when I'm sitting at the kitchen table trying to work on the danged bills. She always did the bookkeeping and taxes. She was good at it. I'm not good at it and I hate it! It's then that she comes back into my head and I begin missing her all over again. I get so blue...and then I start drinking, the bills don't get done and I usually end up with a hangover. Pretty disgusting, huh? It sounds like I don't miss HER...just what she used to do for me...and I KNOW that's not true!"

I agreed that it was not true and knew that at this point it was most important for Tim to understand how *unmet needs* can trigger grief responses and how an entanglement can then exacerbate the grief process. Missing Molly on their evening walks was a real and normal grief response and continuing the walks with his daughters was a good thing. Eventually they might even find different walking trails that they could create for themselves.

I suggested that Tim make a list of the healthy and positive ways he was handling daily tasks. As he read his list out loud, he agreed that he was doing some good and positive things for his daughters and himself.

It was obvious that when it came to the bills, a place where Tim felt totally inadequate, he was getting nowhere in spite of his many attempts. The bills had obviously become a far more significant task than they should have been and it was serving only to throw him further into entangled grief. Every time the bills were in front of him, he reminded himself once more how much he missed his wife. Missing Molly would be one thing. Mixing his grief with the budget and bills would be another thing. While discussing alternatives he might try, he decided to give everything to an accountant once a week. For a period of time, he wouldn't even look at the bills or be bothered or reminded of an obligation he hated and felt inadequate doing. His step-two goal would be to eventually learn how to manage the budget even though it might take a bit of time to get there.

As this scenario ends, be assured that Tim will continue to miss Molly's presence. The *normal* grief response guarantees that this will happen. Hopefully, Tim will be able to use the information he learned about *unmet needs* and be able to recognize if further entanglements begin to interfere with what is already a seemingly unbearable loss situation.

In summary, please remember that it is normal to miss doing the things that you used to do with your loved one and it is normal to miss having the things done for you that the loved one used to do. Be aware of the kinds of resources you will need, now that your circumstances have changed and put them in place before you need them. Otherwise, it would not be unusual that every time something comes up that the other person did for you, you are tossed into an emotional grief response that can easily grow to entanglement proportion.

It will be important to also assess the things you used to do with the person who is no longer with you. Whereas, you may not wish to duplicate those activities exactly, there will be some things you will still want to continue even if in a bit of a different form. In the same way, it will be important to find alternative things to do that will give you pleasure. Even though it may sound a bit rigid, some people benefit by making a list of all of the things one can do alone as well as a list of things to initiate with another person. Sundays can be especially discouraging or depressing after the loss of a loved one, so having the list posted on the refrigerator can serve as a visual reminder.

Even though you will miss times together and you will miss having your loved one with you to do family things you used to do, the *unmet needs* should not continue to be the trigger that reminds you of your loss and/or contributes to prolonging or entangling a grief that is already filled with sorrow.

UNTANGLING FROM
ENTANGLEMENT THREE:
UNMET NEEDS

After the loss of your loved one, and when you feel ready, make a list of all the things that will be very different in your life. (*"Things we did together that I will miss", "Things the person did for me that I will miss", etc.*) Brainstorm all the ways you can strive to meet these needs in healthy ways. For example, if your mate was the one who did all of the household repairs, locate a handy man you can call on and have the phone number ready ahead of time. Plan ahead for days alone and schedule some new activities that will offer some amount of pleasure. I previously mentioned the idea of making a list and posting it on the refrigerator. This can serve as a reminder of things to do when your mind needs to go someplace else and you simply need a diversion. Expand the list of ideas by adding to it as something new comes to mind. We know we cannot fill the absence of the loved one, yet we can be aware of some of the *unmet needs* we will be facing as a result of no longer having this person in our life. This knowledge and action will make a great difference in avoiding a serious entanglement in our already difficult grief process.

A different story of unmet needs brings to mind a lovely lady whose husband died four years prior to her first counseling appointment. June said she couldn't stop missing her husband and felt guilty for thinking about how much she missed going dancing since Bob had died. She talked about going to her closet a few times a week looking at the beautiful dresses and high-heeled shoes she used to wear when they would go ballroom dancing. She went on to share that she sometimes felt angry with Bob for leaving and taking away all of their weekend fun and then she'd feel guilty, knowing that it wasn't Bob's choice to leave. She shared that, at times, her feelings of guilt and upset were often as strong as her feelings of grief.

When asked if she had ever thought about taking a few ballroom dance lessons just to get back into something she loved doing, she said, the possibility of going into a dance environment alone had never crossed her mind, though it was obvious by the look on her face that the thought of it was appealing. June checked back a few weeks later to say she had joined a dance class and was having great fun. She also added that now when she thought of Bob and dancing she was able to smile, knowing that this is exactly what he would be wanting her to do. This is another example of how holding on to an *unmet need* can tangle the grief process and how making just a small lifestyle shift can make a great difference.

Author's note:

I know and understand that all *unmet needs* grief issues will not be able to be solved or corrected as easily as June's story illustrates. Please know however, that I have worked with many, many bereaved people who *have* been able to make a change or two in meeting *unmet needs* and it has worked just as easily as it worked for June in her story.

ENTANGLEMENT FOUR: PERSONAL SENSE OF IDENTIFY BEFORE AND AFTER THE LOSS OF THE LOVED ONE

Each person carries a mental image or picture of him or herself. This image reflects one's feelings of self-worth or self-esteem. The full self-image will take into account a person's various roles (career or job title, husband, wife, mother, father, etc), as well as one's physical attributes, talents, skills and abilities and the person's ability to perceive limitations. Some people tend to limit their sense of identity and value themselves only in regard (for example) to their career or vocation. It isn't difficult to guess what happens when the person retires and no longer has a work-life identity.

In addition to overindulging in a career-related identity, some people tend to have little or no personal identify. Instead, their view of self tends to be connected with another person to whom they have a close relationship. When suddenly or even not so suddenly, the same loved one dies, the bereaved can feel totally lost and alone. An example of this is the widow who describes herself as *"Ed's wife"*. *"I can see now that I saw myself only as an extension of Ed! We did everything together. My whole life was Ed, and now what do I do?"*

Another example is the grieving mother who narrowly defines herself as *"Adam's mom"*. *"I don't even know who I am as Ann Marie. I was so busy being a mom and doing all the things moms do. I have no idea of where to start to find me again,"* she said through tears. It is important to reassure Anne Marie that being there for someone we love is a most admirable quality and it only becomes a problem when one does it to the point that the individual forgets to be there for herself.

Many parents experience this situation to a degree when all of their children leave home and the parents are left to fill their own entertainment card because there are no more sports activities or concerts to attend. One wife relates, *"It was when our last son graduated that I realized that my husband and I really didn't have anything in common anymore. I found myself trying to figure out what I even had in common with myself. All of our time was spent going to athletic events. I can see why we both feel so lost right now!"*

Many times, a person isn't even aware that his or her personal identity has become so intertwined with that of a spouse, child or other individual. It often happens when one person becomes totally involved or dedicated to another, and neglects attending to his or her own personal needs or fails to pursue or develop his own personal interests.

Knowing that this can happen might help one understand how it can significantly impact the grief process and become of *entanglement* proportion. Grief becomes more dramatic because the bereaved is not only experiencing the *earthly miss* of the person who died, the individual is having to rediscover him or herself as well. It can be a lengthy journey to uncover one's own sense of identity after thinking of oneself as *Adam's mom*, or *Ed's wife*, etc. It is a task of untangling, for sure!

Like Anne Marie, you may even be saying to yourself that there are days that you don't know who You are anymore, at least *who you are* separate from the person who is no longer here. Understanding what is involved in one's sense of identity should help you better understand how to find or retrieve your own unique self.

UNTANGLING FROM ENTANGLEMENT FOUR: PERSONAL SENSE OF IDENTITY

This exercise may better explain one's Sense of Identity. Draw three circles and label them as you see them here:

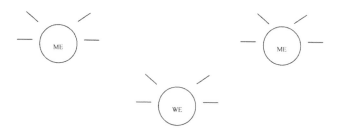

The first *ME* circle represents you. The second *ME* circle represents the person with whom you closely identified and who is no longer here. Imagine the *WE* circle as representing the sum of your relationship as a couple or as a mother and son, or father and son or however it fits with your situation.

Use the webbing technique introduced earlier. As you make strands out from your *ME* circle, jot words that explain who you are as your own person. You may see yourself as a writer, a gardener, a helping person, Bill's wife, Julie's husband, etc. You may come up with words such as independent, overly dependent, enthusiastic learner, etc. Whatever words come to mind, add them all to your circle.

Next, do the same thing for the other person's *ME* circle, thinking of his or her separate and individual qualities or roles that you believe identified that person to him or herself. Finally, write all of the words that tell who the two of you were as a *WE*. You may use words like *work partners, lovers, hike and ski partners, support person, cheerleader,* etc.

If it was your child who died, you may discover that the things in the *WE* circle were all the activities that belonged to your child and you were the support person for these activities. It is easy to see how alone and without identity you might feel if this is your situation. Even if you previously had your own strong sense of who you were independent of your child, you will naturally feel a tremendous void simply because the role of caregiver can become a consuming, yet beautiful task.

Look back at your own *ME* circle. If it has too many responses such as *Bobby's mom, family chauffeur, Bill's wife, etc,* and few qualities that identify you as your own person (*crafts person, pianist, artist, choir member, etc.*), this will help you recognize where you may need to begin. As one begins to recognize the things that can stand in the way of a strong sense of personal identity, consider adding new interests and activities that will add to your sense of identity and slowly but surely bring small pleasures back to life. You will not feel like doing this right after the time of your loss, yet a time will come when you will know that something else is needed. Be gentle, yet firm with yourself as you work to set yourself back on a path towards some new or renewed interests that you can claim as your own.

It will still be a very *normal* grief reaction to continue to miss the life you had with the one who died and it will be a very normal grief reaction to suddenly find yourself in tears because you miss being with, or doing for, the person who is no longer here. Hopefully, however, you will find yourself beginning to slowly respond to the grief as a healthier, stronger and more clearly defined person as you add new pieces to your life. When this begins to happen, it is probable that you will also have a stronger sense of direction in regards to what comes next. I repeat, be gentle and patient with yourself as you make subtle, yet significant changes in your thinking as well as in your activities. Believe that doing so will eventually lead you up and out of this specific grief entanglement.

It bears repeating, to note how important it is for many bereaved individuals to be able to share their thoughts with someone who is willing and knows how to listen. Sometimes that is all we really need in order to sort things out for ourselves. Please do not hesitate to visit about your present sense of identity and ways to expand it with a trained professional. Remember the Identity Circle activity and continue striving to widen and enrich your circle with a mixture of things that better defines who you are.

ENTANGLEMENT FIVE: THE BEREAVED PERSON'S PREVIOUS REACTION PATTERN TO DISAPPOINTMENT, LOSS OR MAJOR CHANGE

If you grew up in a family who avoided talking openly about significant emotional issues such as death, divorce, family conflicts, etc. and if the people in your family of origin dismissed the presence or significance of feelings and emotions such as sadness, disappointment, guilt, etc. you may have unknowingly lost valuable childhood lessons regarding ways of handling and expressing life at the emotional level. How each of us grew up viewing and interpreting the rituals and behaviors of our parents in regard to illness, death, dying and funerals greatly impacts how we will react later in life to similar events.

If your emotional family history matches what I have described, there is a strong chance that when confronted with a serious, personal loss, you may not find it easy to express your sorrow and grief in the ways that might otherwise lead you to a healthier resolve.

On the other extreme, if you grew up in a home where anger, frustration, and disappointment were allowed to go unfettered and fits and tantrums were common expressions, this will also inform your response to grief. Both of these are extremes, so as you trace your own past reaction pattern and when you recall what was modeled for you, you will discover if your present response to grief may be causing you to be stuck in this fifth entanglement.

During a group grief therapy session, a young widow in the group reflected, *"As I look at this entanglement, I can see how it has affected me and how it has definitely kept me 'stuck' since John was killed."* She continued, *"When I was a kid, I was pretty spoiled. I got my way and everything I wanted. I married John and he spoiled me, too. Now, for the first time in my life, things are definitely not going my way and no matter how much I kick and scream, nothing can change the ways things are. It's my guess that this is why I'm having a harder time than I need to right now. The question is, 'what do I do about it?'"*

This woman's present level of maturity (as she looks at her immature responses) and her ability to look at herself in such an honest manner are definite assets in moving away from entangled grief. As is sometimes the case, it took only a few sessions before she was able to adjust her unhealthy, internal dialogue (her *self-talk*) and move into more self-calming and peaceful responses. It goes without saying that being able to change one's *self-talk* takes positive intent and practice. It means correcting oneself when non-productive thinking comes into the mind and substituting with words and thoughts that will move one forward rather than push one down further. The best way to describe it is to think about the words you would like to hear from a best friend and give the same message to yourself.

Making these subtle but significant shifts in thinking doesn't mean she likes the loss anymore than she did before. It means that she has learned that she doesn't need to throw herself into the continued frenzy of anger and emotional outbursts every time she thinks of John.

I will use a personal illustration to show how early family modeling can have such a dramatic impact on future grief situations. As a child, I recall two family members that always wailed at funerals. It frightened me and I also wondered if these people did it to get attention or if they really couldn't help it. At any rate, at that young age, I vowed never to behave in such a way, no matter how I felt. When I was eleven years old, I stopped judging as I sat at my mother's funeral and heard deep, guttural wails releasing from my grandmother as she grieved her only child. The sound of her sorrow was heartbreaking and I knew that she could *not* help herself as she was a very private person and would never have tried to draw attention to herself. All of this frightened me to a degree of unreason and I lived with the constant fear that my grandmother would die from her own grief. As much as I felt my world crumbling, I pushed my feelings deeper and deeper inside, lest they would possibly erupt like hers or the other relatives and fill the space with more of the same chilling sadness and mournful sounds. As you can guess, I grew up with a very unhealthy response to grief. My interpretation of the wailing relatives and my grandmother's uncontrollable grief response was a simple message to me: "Stay in control…either for yourself, or for the good of another person."

I talked to no one about my grief and sadness after my mother's death. Whenever the feelings would get bigger than I could handle, my coping pattern was to take a bath, take a nap, or play the piano. The bath felt soothing and calming. It was my unconscious attempt to cleanse myself both physically and emotionally. The music that my fingers could create on the piano keys offered a calming and a comfort and it gave me the opportunity to momentarily move away from the pain that seemed to forever stir in my heart. The nap was obviously the quickest means of avoiding the thoughts and feelings even if the escape was only for a little while. Whereas, none of my coping choices were harmful, they were all I knew to rely on so I remained *stuck* in the feelings except for short respites. It is clear now that things could have been different if I had felt that I could talk to someone or have help dealing with the deep grief. I'm guessing grief counselors were nonexistent at the time and the people I knew didn't talk much about their feelings.

I believe I was doing the very best that I knew how to do and I feel grateful that my coping mechanisms were not destructive. Responses such as mine, serve only to push the feelings temporarily out of sight. They do not move one towards understanding, acceptance and integration, or a greater sense of peace.

It wasn't until the news of the death of our two sons, who were, as I mentioned before, killed in separate accidents on the same day, that I was finally taken to my knees and all of the pent up grief from *forever* came rolling down on top of me like boulders falling from a steep mountainside. It would be from this heart-wrenching experience that I would slowly ... very slowly ... find my way out of the emotional debris and climb back into sunshine. This would happen only because of my need and my ultimate willingness to face all of the hurt, all of the feelings and emotions related to my losses, both present and from the past.

The *good news* is that even though we become used to thinking and feeling in certain ways...just as I did, our thinking and feeling patterns are pliable and they can change. It happens through awareness (looking and listening to the ways we are thinking and behaving at the present time) and then learning and choosing new ways of thinking and being. Even though the process may seem slow and there may be setbacks along the way, in the long run you will see differences in how you view and react to the events in your life simply because you have chosen to do so. The rewards can be life changing and I am proof that this is true.

The most hopeful solution to healing from the fifth entanglement is to take the time to look at your present responses to loss, disappointment, and grief and to go back and compare them with your childhood patterns of handling such emotions.

UNTANGLING FROM ENTANGLEMENT FIVE: THE BEREAVED PERSON'S PREVIOUS REACTION PATTERN TO DISAPPOINTMENT, LOSS, OR MAJOR CHANGE.

Keep in mind that if we have not had healthy and appropriate developmental experiences of responding to hurt and disappointment as a child, it is easy to carry the same unhealthy patterns and responses into adulthood. *Unhealthy responses* might be observed when a person experiences an emotionally loaded event and the feelings connected with the event are not expressed and are suppressed or camouflaged instead. Be comforted by the fact that it is never too late to learn to respond in new and emotionally healthy ways to disappointing life events. The old adage, *"You can't teach an old dog new tricks"* does not apply to adult human beings as long as awareness and effort are involved.

When I say, *"responding to disappointing life events in new and emotionally healthy ways,"* it means that we are learning and expressing feelings and responses in a more congruent manner when an emotionally laden event occurs in our lives. (If it's a sad event we find the time to cry or express the sadness. If we are disappointed or angry, we are able to communicate the feelings in a way that feels appropriate and not purposefully hurtful to another person.)

This awareness exercise asks us to take a closer look at a specific event. It also allows us to uncover the feelings and emotions connected to that time, and to reexamine our reactions and behaviors to the event.

1. Think of a significant disappointment or loss situation you experienced as a child. Describe it briefly:

2. List all the feelings and emotions you remember having at the time of the disappointment or loss:

3. Describe how you responded (acted and behaved) at the time:

4. Try to recall your feelings and emotions a month or six weeks later:

5. Describe how you responded (acted and behaved) a month or six weeks later:

6. If possible, recall some of your feelings and emotions a year or more after the loss:

7. Describe how you responded (acted and behaved) a year or more after the loss:

Use this same writing format to look at subsequent disappointments and losses that have taken place at different times in your life.

Look over what you have written and see if you can find patterns that describe your reactions to disappointment and grief and loss. Would you consider your responses to be healthy, effective and productive in helping you resolve your loss or do you see your responses as unhealthy and possibly a deterrent to healing? If the latter is true and you feel unable to make new or different responses, please plan to talk to someone you trust who can be of some help. It is probable that when you begin to express your feelings and emotions in a way that is honest and appropriate, you will feel more peace of mind with greater possibility of being able to integrate the loss into your life.

Next Steps in Untangling from Entanglement FIVE:

Pay close attention to what you are saying to yourself in relation to your loss. It can be helpful to write down some of your thoughts so you become more aware of your internal dialogue. Each time you have a thought that feels less productive and not for your *highest good,* mentally *thank* that thought for *sharing* and ask yourself if there is something more nurturing and productive that you might say instead. (Example: *"My life is a total mess since _____ and it's never going to get better!"*)

Produce a new thought that feels lighter and potentially more helpful. Example: *"Whereas, everything feels awful right now. I know these feelings won't last forever."* Say the words to yourself and then say them again. Continue doing this each time the non-productive thinking begins. Listen carefully to any emotional or physical changes that might start to take place. **Your body and mind will begin to relax in direct response to the new messages you are giving it.** The more nurturing the message, the more comforted you will feel.

Reminder: You are not pushing away or totally denying the non-productive thoughts. You are simply choosing not to allow them to have the control and power they have had in the past. The outcome to any event or response changes by changing one's internal response.

This writing exercise will help you become more aware of your internal dialogue (your self-talk) as well as providing new words and messages to tell yourself.

1. A brief description of the upsetting situation:

2. What I am telling myself each time I think about the situation (my self-talk):

3. A new message that I can use in order to be kinder to myself and more self-assuring:

Please trust the value of this process! If you remain dedicated to replacing the new message every time the *gloom and doom* thought comes in to your mind, you will soon begin to experience a more productive and satisfying outcome.

ENTANGLEMENT SIX: THE CONSCIOUS OR UNCONSCIOUS PERSONAL NEED OF THE BEREAVED TO PROLONG THE GRIEF PROCESS

This might be the most difficult of all the entanglements to deal with because of the many different factors involved. It can sometimes be difficult for the grieving person to have the ability and/or willingness to see things in the same rational manner as they might in other circumstances. The thoughts and ideas connected with the sixth entanglement are offered gently because in most all cases, the grieving person's thoughts make sense to him or her at the time. And, in some cases, the reasoning oftentimes rests in the subconscious, away from the person's direct awareness.

Some common internal dialogue connected with this entanglement is:

> *"Letting go of the grief reflects disrespect and/or lack of love for the one who died."*
>
> *"If I stop acting sad, others may think I really didn't care!"*
>
> *"If I let go of the grief, I'm afraid the memory of my loved one will fade or go away completely."*

One very bereaved mother said, *"If my extended family thinks I'm over this, they will expect me to do all of the things I did before Sam was killed, like having Thanksgiving dinner for example, and I just don't want to do that anymore."* In this example, using one's grief to avoid certain expectations or responsibilities only further entangles honest communication as well as time she could be spending in paying tribute to her son by creating a meaningful memorial or simply remembering good things about her son without the other thoughts or excuses interfering. When it was suggested that she could simply say, *"I'd like us to start taking turns having Thanksgiving dinner and I'd rather not do it this year!"* she smiled at the simplicity of the idea.

One mother made daily visits to the grave of her teen-age son who had been killed in an automobile accident. She was still going daily five months after her son's death. She said that in the beginning it comforted her and after a while she thought that if she stopped the ritual she was afraid her son would think she no longer missed him and she wondered also what other people would think if she started doing *fun* things again. As mentioned earlier, this kind of thinking usually makes sense to the bereaved at the time even though it might easily sound like faulty or irrational thinking to others. At a later time it can even seem irrational to the person who was originally having the thoughts.

Letting go of the thinking that causes the sixth entanglement might require the help of a trained professional or a very astute, caring and trusted friend who is willing to listen and reflect back what is being heard in a way that allows the bereaved person to look at the situation differently. As blunt as it might sound, one usually receives an honest answer by responding to the question. *"What is the payoff for me in holding on to these grief behaviors?"* In other words, what happens (and continues to happen) if you hold on to this kind of thinking and behavior, or what might be the consequence if you let go of it? The following writing exercise should offer clarity. Be kind and patient with yourself as you do this work. When we discover that our thoughts and actions are not serving our highest good and may in fact be hindering life as it could be, we can choose to change direction and in doing so, learn to give honest and respectful expression to our grief. At the same time we can learn to set the boundaries that we probably needed to set even before our loved one died.

UNTANGLING FROM ENTANGLEMENT SIX: THE CONSCIOUS OR UNCONSCIOUS PERSONAL NEED OF THE BEREAVED TO PROLONG THE GRIEF PROCESS

Reflect and Write: Answer these questions in as much detail as possible:

Part 1. *How would my loved one want me to be handling this grief? Do I agree with how I think he or she would feel? Explain why or why not.* After responding to Part I, reflect and write about any insights you gained doing this part of the exercise.

Part 2. *What have I observed in how other friends and family members have handled their grief? For how long a period did I see them outwardly grieving?* After responding to these questions, ask yourself if your present way of handling grief is what you are truly feeling or might you be responding in this way because you feel it is expected of you or you don't know what else to do?

Part 3.
What do I think others expect of me in my grief process?

After answering this question, ask yourself if you are meeting your own grief needs or possibly trying to meet what you believe to be, the expectations of others.

Part 4.
Am I consciously or unconsciously using my loss and my grief as an excuse to avoid doing certain things? Ask yourself how you might be more honest with yourself and others and what you wish you could do, or not do instead. Self-honesty is a first step to emotional freedom. From here, it is much easier to learn to set clear boundaries. Too often we tend to think we have to create an excuse for saying *no* to someone's request. Using grief as an *excuse* only contributes to an unnecessary entanglement.

After completing the exercises for the sixth entanglement, if you still feel unsettled or confused about what to do next, do not hesitate to employ the services of a skilled grief therapist. You deserve every chance to heal from your loss in as healthy a manner as possible. As healthy healing occurs, you will be honoring yourself and the loved one who died.

WAYS TO AVOID GRIEF
ENTANGLEMENTS IN
THE FUTURE

As a way of summarizing the six entanglements, we can also look at possible ways to avoid certain unnecessary future grief entanglements. We can be forewarned as we become aware of the six key situations that might potentially cause excess grief and pain.

CIRCUMSTANCES OF THE DEATH

Whereas, we have no control over how the loss of a loved one occurs, we can be aware immediately that if our loss is sudden or traumatic, there undoubtedly will be those specific death circumstances to consider and work through as well as the normal and painful loss of the one who dies. Being aware that *The Circumstances of the Death* definitely factors in to the grief response, one will hopefully be able to look at the two major parts of the loss: the story of how the loved one passed and the grief that always goes with the earthly miss of a loved one.

- If the circumstances of the death are unusual or traumatic, it is wise to seek grief counseling early in order to process the many thoughts and emotions that will be involved.

- If you were present to witness any, or all, of the event, you will definitely benefit from professional help because of the possible post trauma stress issues.

QUALITY OF THE RELATIONSHIP

Being knowledgeable about the second entanglement: *The Quality of the Relationship(s)* is one over which we definitely have some control. By learning and practicing open and honest communication skills, all of our relationships have a great chance of improving. Should the time come when you must say good-bye to a loved one, there will be comfort in knowing that *unsettled business* or thoughts and feelings of guilt do not stand between you and your grief.

Even if you had the very best relationship with the one who died, it is important to keep open and honest communication with all of the people who might be in your grief story. If a friend or relative said or did something that feels hurtful or offensive, or if the doctor or anyone attending your loved one left you feeling frustrated or disappointed, attempt to resolve or mend the relationships. Otherwise, each time you have normal feelings of sadness or thoughts of the loved one who died, the unresolved feelings and emotions attached to the loss can easily become mixed and tangled with the grief.

- Self-help literature such as *"The Dance of Anger"*, *"The Dance of Intimacy"* and *The Dance of Deception* by Harriet Goldhor Lerner, Ph.D. can be most helpful in learning healthy and functional communication skills. I appreciate Lerner's common-sense approach regarding the human nature of relationships. I recommend her books to many of my clients and they usually always comment that her real-life examples and case studies provide an easy to understand means of starting to look at one's own relationships.

When our intent is of goodwill, to and with others, and we have an honest and open pattern of communication the likelihood of becoming enmeshed in the second entanglement is highly improbable.

UNMET NEEDS

One can never predict, for certain, what one's *unmet needs* might be after the loss of a loved one. In my personal situation, I know I would have benefited from learning more of the 'fix-it' and handyman skills that I so easily allowed my husband to do. On the other hand, I realized after he was gone that learning such skills didn't come naturally, nor did I have much interest in learning. It was necessary for me to make a list of my "go-to" people for household repairs and yard work, etc. One could minimize expenses by learning some of those things before hand. I admit that I depend on *Google* to inform me of many things that I don't know about.

Another way to avoid some of the entanglements that can come with *unmet needs* is to develop a stronger sense of independence in your daily life while the people you love are present. This doesn't need to minimize the interdependence that comes with sharing love with another person. It simply suggests that too much dependence on one single person can lead to many *unmet needs* should the person not always be with us.

- Plan ahead! Be as self-sufficient as you can be. Be sure that both marriage partners know how to cook, do laundry, take care of household bills, etc. One person can still be in charge of certain duties though both people should know how to do it! In the same vein, teach your children to cook simple, healthy meals; show them how to do laundry as a first step in becoming self-reliant. It's a good life-skill if nothing else.

- When you feel ready, find a friend to do some of the same things you used to do with the one who died. Whereas, not all of our unmet needs will be met, many can be soothed if we become proactive and reach out to help ourselves.

THE SENSE OF IDENTIFY OF THE BEREAVED BEFORE AND AFTER THE LOSS

- One of the finest ways to gain your own personal sense of identity is to become passionate about something! It might be a hobby, a craft, or it may involve becoming somewhat of an expert on a subject you love. Your sense of achievement will add a strong level of personal accomplishment and your sense of self/identity will be enhanced.

Having a strong sense of identity does not minimize the quality of your special relationships. It does set you apart and also allows you to have some thing or things that are special just to you.

- Practice good self-care. When we take time to exercise, eat right, maintain healthy hygiene, etc. we are showing that we value our body. When we stay informed by reading, taking classes and learning new things we are showing respect for our mind. When we take time to enjoy nature and the outdoors, we nurture the spirit. All of these practices add to a stronger sense of identity and in turn, we naturally feel more in tune with our inner self.

THE BEREAVED PERSON'S PERSONAL REACTION PATTERN TO LOSS OR MAJOR LIFE CHANGE

- Today…right now…start to become aware of your present reactions to disappointment and loss. If you recognize that having a *melt-down* is a common response when even small things go wrong in your daily life, you may wish to reevaluate your responses to various situations. Cognitive Behavioral Therapy operates on the premise that each of us is capable of changing our response to a situation. The change is initiated by first listening to our *self-talk* (what we are saying to ourselves) about a given situation. Once we start to change the message in our head to a more positive response, the outcome will change as well. Research shows that people with a higher degree of *hardiness* are those that have more optimistic and calming responses to external events.

If we have formed the thinking habit of *awful-izing* or going in to panic mode when something goes wrong or disappoints us, we can expect to be devastated when something truly major happens to us. Please know that when we lose a person, it is normal to feel total devastation and sorrow. However, people who have formed negative thinking responses to smaller life-events are at far greater risk of being plagued with the fifth entanglement. I say this gently but if you or someone you know has grown up forever throwing temper tantrums when something goes wrong, one might expect a similar temper tantrum when a significant loss comes into his or her life. Knowing that we cannot reverse the permanent loss of a loved one ultimately requires an acceptance of that truth.

- Practice changing your responses! Become familiar with the equation: E+R=O.

Event + Response= Outcome. The Event cannot be altered (it's already happened). The *Response* to the *Event* can be changed when one chooses to view it in a different way. When we change our Response, the Outcome changes. We begin by practicing with the smaller happenings: When you are at a STOP sign or red light, instead of tapping your foot or feeling anxious about having to wait, tell yourself something that will change the impatient response such as *"It's not the end of the world. I can take a few moments to breathe deeply."* When someone cuts in front of you, instead of feeling angry or impatient, try for a different and possibly humorous response. . . *"He must be in a bigger hurry than me!"* When someone backs out of a social date at the last minute, choose to forgive and let it go rather than extend the feelings of disappointment or anger to the place of ruining the rest of your day. As you practice changing your responses to different situations and events, you will feel happier and more at peace. This doesn't mean that permanent loss is going to be *a piece of cake* if and when you have to face it. It isn't easy for anyone. It does mean that you will probably have an easier time of facing the situation and in time you will be more readily able to accept, with grace, what has taken place.

THE CONSCIOUS OR UNCONSCIOUS PERSONAL NEED OF THE BEREAVED TO PROLONG THE GRIEF PROCESS

- Be true to yourself rather than choosing to believe you have to live up to the expectations of others in regard to your personal grief response. People differ in grief expression. Some prefer to get back to a *normal* schedule sooner than others. Just because other friends or family members did something a certain way, doesn't mean it's the best way for you. Resuming your normal activities does not have to send the message to others that you are over your grief and it doesn't denote the degree of love that you felt for the one who died.

- Don't expect others to know how you think or feel. If you want someone to know how you feel, tell the person. Most people don't know what to do or say to help a bereaved friend or relative. Rather than only feeling sad and isolating yourself in order to relay the message that you are in deep grief, share honestly if you need help or need to talk to someone. If you truly wish to be left alone and not bothered, relay this as well (though I hope these feelings don't last for too long a time).

- Refuse to allow your grief to serve as an excuse to avoid doing something that you really didn't want to do in the first place. This takes us back to healthy thinking and healthy communication. As an example, if you do not feel up to hosting the annual holiday dinner at your house as you usually do, that is understandable. If, on the other hand, you've been trying to get out of it for a couple of years and now you use your grief as an excuse, you are not being honest with yourself or others. In addition, behaviors such as this will probably interfere with what might have been a healthier grief aftermath.

Knowledge of the six different grief entanglements and how they occur will hopefully serve as a gentle guide in moving you, or someone you love, closer to a healthy grief resolve. Knowing some ways to avoid an entanglement in the first place will possibly lead you to a fuller and happier life as well as a softer ending when someone dies.

AFTER CARE: PERSONAL
THOUGHTS FROM THE
AUTHOR

I wish I could spend some time with each one of you who have read and *worked* your way through this book. Hopefully, you have discovered and understood some of the reasons for how and why we can become *stuck* in our grief. I hope there has been new awareness to help you gain greater clarity of vision in regard to some of the thoughts and behaviors related to your loss. Clarity of vision leads us to *right answers*. Though answers may be different for each of us, they must nonetheless become clear within the mind of each person.

Honor your grief. By this, I mean find a way that allows you to honor the person who died and at the same time pay tribute to your feelings. Some people find comfort in giving a book to the library each year in memory of their loved one. One person I know well, honors her daughter, who passed at a young age, by taking a day off from work on the child's birthday. She gives herself time to reflect, and think about the beautiful four years they had together.

There are many ways that one can choose to honor and pay tribute to a loved one that has died; on the other hand, honor and tribute can simply be a function of the heart that no one but you knows about. The main thing is to listen to, and honor what feels best for you.

Self-care, after the loss of a loved one.
This is an important time to look at, and expand your personal self-care program. Whereas, the early stages of grief or emotional trauma are natural times for the mind and the body to quiet and repair themselves, there comes a time when we may need to give the mind and body a boost by moving into something that has the potential to offer new light and energy. If, after an extended period of time, you continue to lack energy, feel depressed, and find yourself filled with more sadness than you care to deal with on a daily basis, listen to your body and take note of some of the following thoughts:

What are you eating and drinking?
Be sure that you are eating a well balanced diet even if it may consist of less food than you have eaten in the past. Green leafy veggies and fruits, fish, beans and whole grains are a must for helping our mental and emotional states. You may find that taking a B vitamin supplement will contribute to

clearer thinking and improved emotional wellbeing. If you are consuming large amounts of caffeine, soda or alcohol, you will not be as physically, mentally or emotionally alert. You may wish to reduce consumption of these items, or eliminate them altogether.

Getting Back Into Things After a Period of Time

Research shows that exercise (walking, working out, swimming, etc.) raises serotonin levels in the brain. Serotonin is a natural brain chemical that allows us to think and behave in a more calm and positive manner. Low levels of serotonin contribute to depression. We know also that lively and energetic music raises serotonin levels in the brain. If, and when it feels right, try fast walking with headphones and some favorite peppy music. Be sure you are aware of the traffic pattern where you are walking, as the music may serve as a distraction. Know that I am not suggesting fast walking and peppy music as a grief-distracter, nor as something that will serve well if your grief is new. Simply be aware of the power of music to either energize or to soothe and use it as you need it and when you need it.

Thoughts on singing and laughter...

Please know that I am not offering singing and laughter as an antidote for early grief. You may have already discovered that when you have feelings of sadness or when grief is new, and you try (for example) to sing a hymn in church or at a memorial gathering, tears appear. The same can happen when a certain song is playing on the radio and reminds you of a person or a special time. Music can be the trigger for tears.

On the other hand, singing and laughter has the capability of changing brain chemistry in the same way that exercise does. Both are powerful agents for emotional change when the time comes that one longs to be able to feel something other than total sadness. Maybe it seems so long since you have laughed that you wonder if you ever will again. Consider renting a funny movie, if for no other reason than to be reacquainted with the sound of your own laughter. Your deceased loved one would love to hear your laughter! Possibly imagine the person smiling and offering you a nod and a total look of encouragement.

Spend time with other people. . .

Was the person who died the one with whom you spent the majority of your spare time doing things together? Regardless of one's answer, maybe it's time to find a small group of people who share some of your interests. Some people benefit greatly from the right grief support group. Being able to talk openly and share stories about your loved one can be healing. At the same time, it is an opportunity to hear others share how they are coping with loss. On the other hand, some people say that going too soon after the loss is too painful. One client's words help us understand: *"I had enough pain of my own. I simply couldn't go listen to others cry and tell their stories."* Be sensitive and aware of what fits best for your situation.

After a time, you may wish to consider broadening your interest base or reacquainting yourself with a hobby or interest you used to enjoy doing. Believe it or not, cooking is therapy for some people, so getting back into the kitchen and cooking for friends or a neighbor might be good for all involved. There are even culinary groups that meet and share kitchen enthusiasm.

The idea is to look for and spend time with like-minded people, or people who may introduce you to new ways of thinking and doing. In the process, doors may open for other things. Loneliness after loss is one of the pieces of life that is difficult to endure, though it need not be there forever. The task of looking for something new to add to life may at first feel a bit contrived. When ready, I urge you to persevere. Possibly a book group would be a good fit. Camaraderie and mental stimulation can be a boost for the blues. If you appreciate and benefit from physical activity you may enjoy joining an organized group of hikers, bikers or runners... whatever activity suits you best. The main thing is to take a good long look at what you are doing now, access what might add a bit of zest to your life and be willing to take the necessary steps forward.

If none of the ideas are appealing, possibly a short-term grief support group *would* be beneficial. The point is to get yourself moving towards something that will help revive the spirit after a longer than usual period of grief.

Volunteer

Volunteer work provides a means of being in contact with people, while at the same time, it offers valuable help to an individual, a group, or an organization. Giving and doing for others has extreme healing power. As we light a candle in the life of another, our own light naturally brightens.

Nature is a natural healer!

Outside my kitchen window in my Wyoming home, I had what I called my *spirit spot.* I would tend this small fenced in space with love and devotion and in return, beautiful flowers graced the area throughout our short growing season. It was also the place where birds, butterflies and not-too-hungry bunnies would come to visit. After the sudden accidental death of our grandson, Andy, my spirit spot became my place of quiet retreat; the place to go to think and write my thoughts, cry my tears and feel the comfort of nature hold and embrace me. I would encourage you to consider creating such a spot either in your yard or in a special piece of nature that you can at least adopt and call your own. Creating a small flower or vegetable garden also allows us to be close to the earth as we tend it on our hands and knees and offer thanks for the abundance that does exist in our now new and different life.

Hiking familiar mountain trails and sharing the places in nature that we had shared with Andy was another form of solace. Similar comfort might come in the form of a walk in the woods, sitting by a lake or the ocean or perched atop a mountain lookout. Wherever you are, nature is close by. Find it and let it hold and comfort you!

These are only a few suggestions to get you thinking about what might be the best direction for you to take right now. One thing for sure is that if we keep on doing *the same thing*, we will probably keep on getting *the same results*, so making a change and giving something new a good try may be the move that takes us in a sunnier direction.

It is my opinion that bereavement really is a lifelong journey and it becomes a *part* of who we are, though it does not, and should not *define* us. We are not our grief and our sorrow. We are the result of having lived through the grief and sorrow.

Many of you may be finding that the pieces are coming together again and the sun shines more than it is cloudy and the rain lasts for shorter periods of time. To each of you, I say, *"Brave Warrior!"* I know the journey has not been an easy one!

And, if the pieces haven't yet come together, Hold On, Beloved! Believe and trust in yourself and your Higher Power! Both will be there for you in whatever way or ways you need.

I remember when I thought I would never be able to go on and that life would never feel happy or complete again. I recently came upon a piece of writing that I entered in one of my journals. I wrote it as I was finally passing through a black and bleak grief period.

> *"I moved away from time and space as I knew it*
> *In my everyday world and I did it as often as I could.*
> *Not so much from conscious effort. . .*
> *More from an inner calling. . .a knowing of sorts*
> *That if I were ever to regain a recognizable part of me,*
> *It would be through the arms of nature, that would*
> *Hold me, heal me and bring me back.*
> *Even better: a different person would be returning".*

The person that *returned* still sometimes wonders what it would have been like if she would have grown up with a birth mother as most children do. And, tears still appear unannounced when she thinks of those she loved so dearly, and who left way too soon.

I am filled with deep gratitude, both for the woman that *was*, and the woman that *is* now. I am grateful that these thoughts do not consume me as they once did. By carrying the beautiful memories of earthly times together, the weight of the grief has softened and the heart has opened once again. I am convinced that this is the path of the Spirit.

Blessings on each of you!
May love and light shine on you…
And THROUGH you!!

ACKNOWLEDGEMENTS

I have deep appreciation for the many clients who lovingly and openly share their grief stories and courageously find their way through many of the entanglements in search of inner peace. I am privileged to have been with many of them on their journey. All names and stories have been altered to protect confidentiality except for Anna's Story and my own personal stories.

I wish to thank the many people who encouraged and supported this work. My family, close friends and clients have been enormous encouragers. I am grateful for the talented Create Space staff. They patiently held my hand through the publishing process and were the best listeners in the world!

I offer sincere thanks to those who read or offered time and support for the manuscript: Joy Johnson, Carol Shonka, Lois Olson, Kate Stephens, Carrie Pinsky, my daughters Kathleen Beebout, Julie Varner and Kimberly Allen, my granddaughter,

Anna Mitton and others that I may be neglecting to mention. A special thank you to Christie Anderson and she knows why.

I am eternally grateful to my granddaughter Andrea Beebout, who offered endless support and patiently mentored me through one technical issue after the other. My thanks also to William Peterson, my next-door neighbor who stepped in each time I asked for his technical help.

Since beginning to write this labor of love, my life partner has passed on. He was the trusted person who listened to me tell my early childhood grief story over and over. It was through this ritual of telling the story, shedding the tears and then telling it again, that the bereaved child within slowly began to heal. After the death of our sons, and later, the loss of two of our grandchildren, we were partners in grief as we understood and held each others pain as no one else could. I continue to hear his words of encouragement for this work and I thank him for the belief he had in me at times when I didn't believe in myself.

I am filled with gratitude for the words of encouragement and unconditional love shown to me by my maternal grandparents, Ida and Clarence Clark.

Author's note: Please feel free to contact me at <u>sharongr104@ aol.com</u>.

I welcome your thoughts and will appreciate knowing if even one idea offered here has been of help to you.

22826015R00061

Made in the USA
Lexington, KY
15 May 2013